Matthew Perry

Matthew Perry dated Julia Roberts and suffered from drug addiction. And the doctors expected him to die.

His Childhood

Born in Williamstown, Massachusetts, on 19 August 1969. His mother Susan Marie Morrison was a Canadian journalist and former press secretary to Canadian Prime Minister Pierre Trudeau, and his father John Bennett Perry was an American actor and former model.

His parents divorced before his first birthday, and his mother subsequently married journalist Keith Morrison, and he stayed with her and her husband in Ottawa where he studied there. During his adolescence, Matthew Perry took more interest in sports than acting, especially in tennis and became a junior player, finishing in the top spots in competitions at the time.

His practical successes

In 1994, when he was not known as an actor, he was accepted to star in Friends, which lasted from 1994 until 2004 for 10 years.

During this period and each season, Matthew Perry gained greater fame, acting performances, presentation of programmes and very large funds, with his accruals in the popular series only reaching over $1 million per episode.

Besides starring in the television series, Matthew Perry appeared in a number of films, including Fools Rush In (1997), The Whole Nine Yards (2000), and (2009) 17Again.

The author, writer and producer also participated in the comedy series Mr. Sunshine, which ran from February to April 2011. In August 2012, Matthew Perry played Ryan King, the sports host of Go On and the series was cancelled on 10 May 2013, and also co-starred in The Odd Couple.

His love life

In 1995, Matthew Perivi entered into a relationship with actress Jasmine Blythe, but this relationship did not last, and in late 1995 he dated famous actress Julia Roberts, and remained with her until 1996.

After about 10 years, he did not enter into a serious relationship, until he was associated with Elizabeth Kaplin for 6 years, from 2006 until 2012.

In 2021 Matthew announced his engagement to his beloved Molly Horowitz after he had dated her for two years and revealed the event to People magazine, saying, "I decided to get engaged, because I'm dating the greatest woman on the planet at this time."

Matthew Perry, American actor, born August 19, 1969, Williamstown, Massachusetts. His father moved to Ottawa, Ontario, so he has both Canadian and American citizenship, and is the son of United States actor John Perry. He has been playing tennis since he was 15, he has never had his name Sami. He played Chandler Ping at Friends, and he's the youngest of them. His father acted with him in Fools rush in his father's role and also appeared in an episode of Friends as Gashua's father one of Ritchell's friends. Over the course of his life, he was subjected to many accidents, the first of which took place when he lost part of his middle finger from his right hand while he was young. In 2000, he collided with his B. M ' You can see the effect this incident left on his forehead. He was also injured while playing the racket in his face - you can see the impact of this incident on his chin, you will find it different from what it was. He was suffering from pain in his mouth due to the tooth of the mind, overusing painkillers which led to her addiction.

careerism

At the age of 15, Bree moved from Ottawa to Los Angeles to be represented by Buckley School in Sherman Oaks and graduated in 1987. He acted at the Improvisational Theatre at the Connection Theatre in Los Angeles while still in high school. He played Chaz Russell in the series Second Chance After the 13th Episode Pumped Up The Boys Will Still Be Boys and the Plot became focused on Chaz and his teenage friends. After the first and only part of the series, he stayed in Los Angeles and filmed the first Villac to take part in 1988 [Night in Jimmy Riardon's Life on] in 1989. While doing several guest roles, Brie came forward to play a regular role in CBS Ceden's Sitcom, and played Valery Bertenley's younger character. In 1991, he appeared as a guest at Beverly Hills, 90210 Roger Azarian. He won his TV role in ABC Free Home's sitcom, which aired 11 episodes, followed by Lax 2194?

He tried to secure an audition in the six-from-one series then named Friends by Marta Moffman and David Cran, who had previously worked with them on Dream On, despite the fact that he was committed to filming Lachs 2194 and did not initially consider conducting an audition. When he read the script he got the role of Chandler Bing.

The Friends series was a landslide success, and Brie and his co-workers became global stars - which he aspired to, as he told The New York Times, "There was steam coming out of my ear, I wanted to be very famous. The program brought him a nomination for the 2002 Emmy Award for Best Actor in a Comedy Series, alongside Matt LeBlanc, but they lost it to Ray Romano. Brie appeared in the fools rushing with the participation of his father John Pry and Salma Al Hayek, and almost three heroes to the entire nine-yard tango (with Bruce Willis and his part Tanny's 10 full responses and a good service.

While he was best known mainly for his comedy roles, Brie also played dramatic roles, most notably the role of White House Assistant Counsel Joe Quincey in writer Aaron Sorkin's West Wing series and earned him a three-time appearance in this series (twice in the fourth and once in the fifth) as a nominee for the Emmy Uncle Guest Role Awards in a drama series in 2003 and 2004. Perry is referred to in the show before his guest - Donna Moss searches for him (off screen) in the episode "20 Hours in Los Angeles." He also appeared as lawyer Todd Merrick in two episodes at the end of the fifth part of Ally Shackled including a special two-hour watch aimed at reviving comedy - legal drama.

After completing the filming of [Friends of the American Series], Friends of Prey started his first directorial experiment in an episode in the fourth part of the series Scrabs, and appeared as Murray Mark, operator of the traffic control team at a small airport. He is asked to donate his kidney to his father Gregory (done by his real father)

He also starred in Ron Clark's story film, produced by the Turner Television Network, known as "Triumph" and satisfied on 13 August 2006. Barry played the role of small-town teacher Ron Clark who teaches the most difficult class in the country and Barry received the nomination of Golden Globe and Amy for his performance. [Need a source]

From 2006 to 2007, Brie appeared in Aaron Sorkin's Studio 60 series on Sun Set Strip and Brie played Matt Albee with Bradley Whitford's side, playing Danny Tipp, a duo who muttered from a writer and director trying to save a series of short scenes from failure.

Some felt that Brie's role was based on Sorkin's personal experiences, especially on television.

Perry in 2010

In 2006, he began filming Psychedelic, a film that tells the story of a man with a disturbing personality disorder. The film was delayed several times, but was released to DVD on May 13, 2008. Matthew also appeared in David Mamt's sexually perverse film in Chicago in London. In 2009, mature Dole Mike O'Donnell played in 17 again. In 2008 he starred in the bizarre Birds of America, playing Maurie Tanagher, a nervous man who had to deal with his brothers. He also participated in a series produced by Showtime based on the series End of Steve, a black comedy starring, writing and producing with Peter Tolan.

In 2011 he starred in the comedy series Sid Sunshine, based on Bree's original idea for work and produced by ABC. Barre was assigned the role of a middle-aged man with a crisis of identity. But ABC canceled the series after nine episodes. On 1 March 2012, news of Prey's signing starring in the new NBC comedy series continued to be written and produced by Friends writer Scott Silver. Filming began in May 2012, Brie played Ryan King, a sports presenter trying to skip his wife's death with the help of mandatory Allak sessions. The series premiered on 8 August 2012 as a "premiere" after the 2012 Summer Olympics. The series was shown on September 11, 2012. On 2 October 2012, NBC ordered a full season of 22 episodes. In May 2013, NBC canceled work shortly after the end of the first season. In 2012, Brie appeared as a guest actor in the series produced by CBC The Good Wife and played Mike Christeva, a lawyer, and in 2013 he appeared again in Part IV.

In 2014, he first took part in a British dog-thrower series that featured as part of Sky Arts Play House Priznets. He played a "guy with a Creasma" who charmed the dog by throwing his dog in the air. From 2015 to 2017, he starred in and co-wrote the odd duo and was also an executive producer and offered work on CBS. Bree played Osker Madison in front of Thomas Lannon, who played Flex Unger.

Brie starred in the play End of Suspension, which premiered at the Playhouse Theatre in London. The work was moved to Broadway Gee Theatre MC Sen and was inaugurated on 5 June 2017 with the participation of Jennifer Morrison.

In March 2017, he again played Mike Christva in The Good Foot and is affiliated with The Good Wave.

Later in 2017, he played Ted Kennedy in the miniseries Al Kennedy: After Camlot.

In 2018, Business Insider reported that Barre's wealth was worth nearly $80 million.

In December 2020, he suspended his participation in Cameo's video platform.

Bree launched his survey merchandise from The Friends before the reunion episode was screened.

Bree has Canadian and American citizenship. Brie dated Jasmine Blythe in 1995, and also dated Julia Roberts from 1995 to 1996. Matthew had to write a quantum physics research and present it to Roberts to persuade her to appear in the series Friends. Bree also dated Lizzie Kapolen from 2006 to 2012.

Brie is a fan of the video game series [[Bean Ott (Series) ★ Bean Ott. When he appeared on an episode of Ellen DeGeneres Show, a copy of Bean Ott 3 encouraged the game's studio to give him the new version of Bean Ott: New Vgas in August 2018, there was news about Prey performing stomach surgery to treat an intestinal infectious hole. On 15 September 2018, he stated in a tweet, he spent three months recovering in the hospital after his operation in June 2018. He addressed Molly Horvitz, a literary director, in November 2020. Rumours had spread in December 2019 about him dating him, after two Christmas spends together.

Prescription addiction

In 1997, Perry ended a 28-day program to recover from Vicodin's addiction. His weight was noticeably fluctuating over the ensuing few years, dropping to 145 kg, and losing 20 kg in 2000 to pancreatitis. In February 2001, he entered a rehabilitation centre to recover from Vicodin addiction, Methadone and Amphetaminatol alcohol. While filming the film Service Sarah in Texas, he experienced acute stomach pain and went to Los Angeles for examination at Daniel Freeman Hospital in Marina del Rey, California. His business manager Lisa Castler confirmed that he had entered a rehabilitation centre: Bree then stated that because of addiction problems he did not remember three years while filming a series of Friends, "The period between Season 3 and 6." In 2011, as a celebrity spokesperson for the National Association of Drug Court Professionals, Bree went to Capitol Hill to invite members of the Congress to support the financing of drug courts. In May 2013, Perry was awarded the Hero of Recovery Award by the White House Office of National Anti-Drug Policy for opening Manole Perry, a sober living house in his former mansion in Malibu, California.

In 1997 Matthew Perry struggled with his addiction to the drug Vicodin, dropping his weight dramatically and reaching 66 kilograms, as a result of suffering from pancreatitis.

In February 2001, he entered a centre, to get rid of his Vicodin and alcohol addiction, came out after a while, and in 2011 Matthew Perry became a celebrity speaker for the National Association of Drug Court Professionals, although he did not get rid of his addiction.

In August 2018, Matthew Berrelle underwent abdominal surgery to repair a gastrointestinal perforation, and on 15 September 2018, he revealed that he had spent 3 months in hospital to be treated.

In July 2019, the world media reported that Matthew would not live for more than 6 months, having increased in weight by about 50 pounds, no longer concerned with his health and personal hygiene, due to his drug addiction, and his gloomy state prevented him from acting as a mature and conscious man.

According to his colleagues Courteney Cox and Jennifer Aniston, they tried to communicate with him, but he did not respond to their contacts. In medical analysis reported by the Hollywood newspapers, it was reported that in the case of Gemathio Perrez as such and avoiding treatment, he would not live more than 6 months of the day!

The actor knew he needed help.

Shortly after the accident, the comedian knew that his dependence on drugs had become abnormal. He asked for help in rehabilitation center in Minnesota. Matthew described the 28 days he spent rehabilitating the Hazelden Foundation as' the scariest I've ever had '.
However, his drug problems were far from over. According to Berry, sober was a rigorous process, one that required more than four weeks.
Rules made difference
More urgent than the palliative star's addiction was his alcoholism. He revealed that he was often hidden, during his tenth consecutive year of 'Friends', but Perry set a rule for himself, to prevent his individuals from discovering his secret problem. Drinking on set was a 'no' for him, no matter how much he wanted to do it.

The moment Matthew broke this one rule, he found out it was time to save himself. The legendary star recalled drinking uncontrollably, during filming, while filming 'Service Sarah', which prompted his decision to change.

A second chance at life

In 2001, the 49-year-old returned to rehabilitation; This time in Los Angeles. There is a handling of his alcoholism and drug addiction. This time, the Friends star was determined to defeat his demons before leaving him. Finally, he became sober, reintegrating back into society, with a new determination to maintain sobriety.

Did the entire episode go unnoticed?

Although he tried to keep his drinking excesses from the media and his colleagues, some of the friends involved still noticed. The majority referred to his illness status and advised him to seek assistance. The act was evident in its volatile weight and separate appearance. After his triumphant recovery, his friends and commissioners were very happy to see him back to his good self.

New Start

After the unpleasant addiction battle, the NBC star decided to put other struggling addicts on their way to recovery. He was awarded the Champion of Recovery Award in 2013 from the U.S. National Drug Control Policy, for his efforts to curb drug addiction.

To show his loyalty to the cause, the winner of the heroic award transformed his Malibu home into a sober living facility for men.

Not the last

Between his good deeds and consistent preventive rehabilitation sessions in subsequent years, the scars of an unhealthy past continue to haunt him. In 2017, Matthew revealed that he suffers from acute pancreatitis, a condition caused by the indiscriminate consumption of drugs and alcohol.

In line with this, the 49-year-old symbol underwent emergency surgery to repair the rupture of the digestive tract, also as a result of a previous addiction. Perry's journey is indeed a wonderful one and serves as a motivation for many in a similar situation, but needless to say, the drug-free goal of the representative is still being advanced; One full of ups and downs.

"About love, friendship and crises.." "Friends" star Matthew Perry brings up his memory and reveals the secrets of his life and the scenes of the famous series

Matthew Perry's plan to recount his experiences

In the same vein, a source told US Weekly last February that Matthew Perry was looking forward to retelling his experiences. Whether it's good or bad, to help others and set the record straight about a number of incidents that have been either untold so far, They have been taken out of their true context, or in some cases completely twisted in the wrong way and need to be fully clarified.

The source added: "He will delve deeper into his addiction, as well as clarifying rumours about his feelings for his" Friends "colleagues, as well as discussing errors in a number of his past relationships, he will also discuss what it was like in his life and work, whether good or bad."

Matthew Perry's plan to recount his experiences

In the same vein, a source told US Weekly last February that Matthew Perry was looking forward to retelling his experiences. Whether it's good or bad, to help others and set the record straight about a number of incidents that have been either untold so far, They have been taken out of their true context, or in some cases completely twisted in the wrong way and need to be fully clarified.

The source added: "He will delve deeper into his addiction, as well as clarifying rumours about his feelings for his" Friends "colleagues, as well as discussing errors in a number of his past relationships, he will also discuss what it was like in his life and work, whether good or bad."

The actor publicly admitted at the time that he had suffered a perforated digestive tract, having already spent weeks fighting for his life after his colon exploded from overusing opioids, spending two weeks in a coma and five months in hospital and having to use a bag for nine months.

When he first entered the hospital, he says: "Doctors told my family I had a 2 percent chance of living, I put on something called an ECMO machine, which does all the breathing for your heart and lungs, nobody survives that."

When Perry first appeared in Friends aged 24, his alcoholism was just beginning to appear, he remembers: "I could have sort of dealt with it, but when I became 34, I was really addicted and things got out of hand, but there were years when I put things back under control during that time season nine was the year when I was out of addiction and it was the season when I was nominated for best actor, he should have told me something. "

At one terrifying stage during his time on Friends, Perry was taking so many drugs that it affected his weight and a noticeable shortage, he said: "I didn't know how to stop, even if the police came to my house and said if I drank tonight, we would take you to prison, the first thought that came to mind was to pack up because I definitely would spend a night in prison, I couldn't stop because disease and addiction got worse, it got worse as you got older."

Although Perry tried to hide his condition, the dramatic changes in his appearance each year reflect his state of addiction, and adds that his cast mates were understanding, patient.

Frank about his setbacks - he has rehabilitated 15 times over the years - Perry became well aware of the tools needed to keep him from drinking, he said before joking: "I'm healthy, I shouldn't go to the gym much more, because I don't want to be able to play superheroes, but I'm a man who's healthy right now."

While he prefers not to disclose how long he has spent without drinking currently, he still counts every day, saying: "It's important, but if you lose your commitment, it doesn't mean you lose all that time you've spent learning, sometimes things change, but that's all that changes, you'll still know everything you knew before, as long as you're able to keep going and fight on the way back without dying, you'll learn a lot."
He also said that he also had scars: he had 14 surgery on his abdomen so far, saying: "There are a lot of reminders to stay out of addiction, all I have to do is look down."
As for his motivation to stop using drugs, Perry recalls: "My therapist said, next time you think about taking a drug, just think about colon piercing and you're going to have to use a bag for the rest of your life, so I don't want to use any anaesthetic anymore."

Because Ann Perry is more determined than ever to try to help others suffering from addiction as well, he says: "There were five people put on an ECMO machine that night and the other four died and survived, so the big question is why? Why were you me? there must be some kind of reason ".

For those who will read the book: "I think they will be surprised how bad it is at certain times and how close I am to death. I say in the book that if I actually die, people will be shocked. But no one would be surprised, and that's so scary to live with. So I hope people deal with it, and they know that this disease attacks everyone. no matter if you are successful or unsuccessful, the disease does not care ".

When it comes to gratitude for being alive, Perry learned that: "Everything starts with commitment, because if you don't have an obligation, you can't do anything, so I'm a very grateful man. I'm grateful to be alive, that's for sure. This gives me the possibility to do anything. "

He insists that the trip, despite being incredibly black at times, made him stronger in all respects, says: "What struck me most is my resilience, the way I can recover from all this pain torment, and the desire to tell the story, although it's a little scary to tell all your secrets in a book, but I didn't leave anything, everything is there."

Matthew Perry's great roles as well as friends

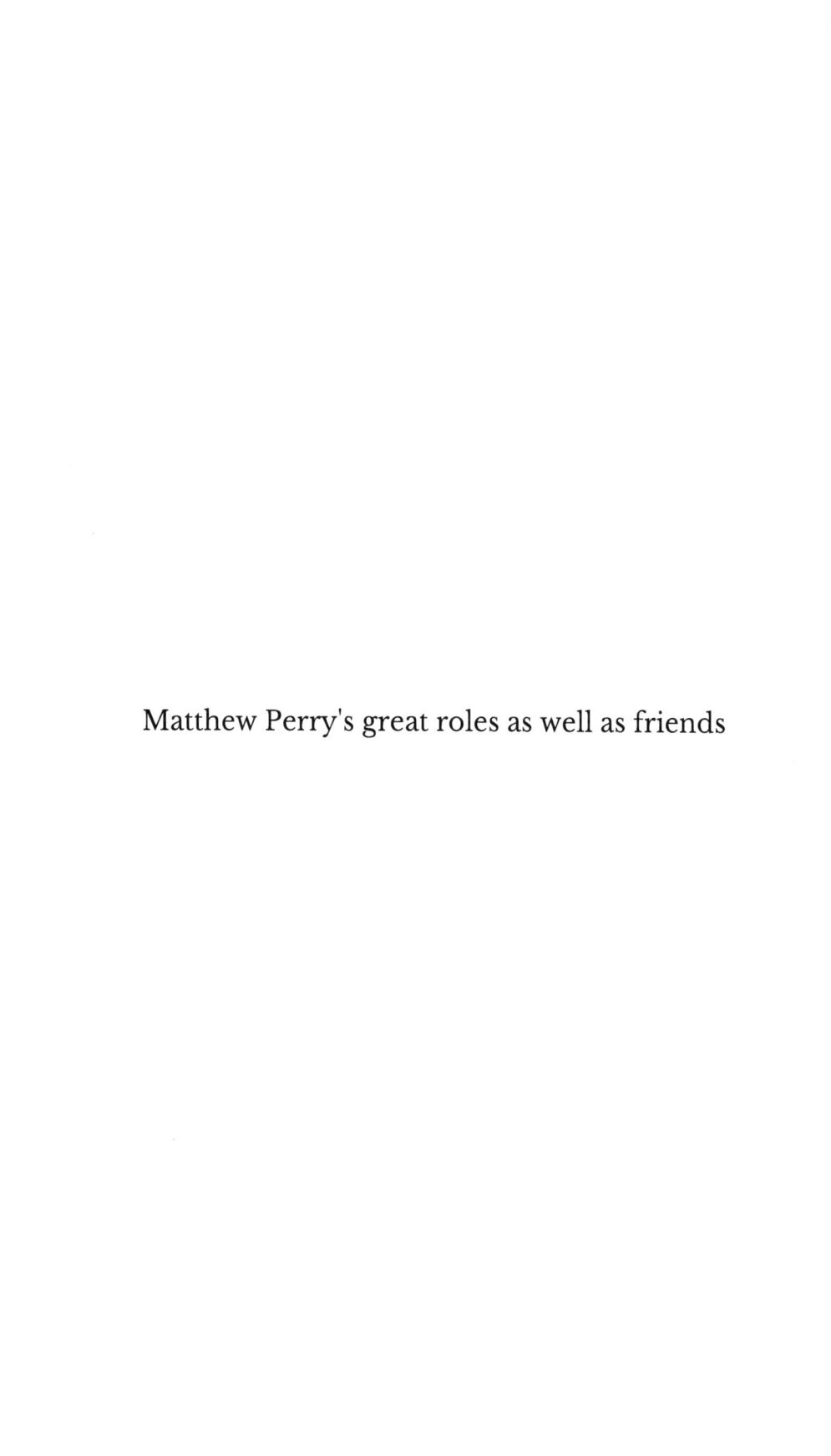

Matthew Perry - We all know him as Chandler Ping, Chan-Chan Man, Miss Chanandler Bong in the sitcom Friends. His role in one of the greatest TV shows he knew, in thick and thin. Chandler Ping will probably forever be Matthew Perry's most iconic role because he filmed the character for 10 full seasons, and did a great job of it. However, throughout his career, Perry naturally took on other roles, both on the small screen and the big screen. Today, we take a closer look at Matthew Perry's eight outstanding roles along with the one that made him a star. In 1997, his third season was a great success, Matthew Perry is already a huge star with a number of nominations and awards under his belt, and he received the first starring role in a film. Besides Salma Hayek, Perry starred in the romantic comedy Fools Rush In.

Now, this is not a film that deserves an award by any means. It's a game rom-the-the-mill with Perry like Alex Whitman, a nightclub builder who has a one-night stand with aspiring photographer Isabel Fuentes (Hayek) leading to an unexpected pregnancy. They decided to keep the baby healthy. Rush. It's a fun enough movie with Matthew Perry's baby face that brandishes its distinctive kind of magic and humor.

The acclaimed medical comedy series Scrubs featured many interesting guest stars, including Matthew Perry. In 2004, Perry appeared as a guest on the fourth season of Scrubs in an episode entitled "My Unicorn." Perry played Murray, the son of a JD patient who needed a kidney transplant.
However, because his father was not as present as he needed and because he gave him the "name of an old man," Murray was reluctant to help. In the end, it was revealed that Gregory is not his biological father but Murray gives him a kidney anyway because he was a "decent father" nonetheless. The episode was directed by Matthew Perry, whose father John Bennett Perry played Gregory.
Cougar Town is a 2009 sitcom starring Courteney Cox, nicknamed Monica from Friends, such as Jules Cobb - a newly divorced woman in her 40s who faces humorous experiences, pitfalls and rewards in her new life with her son and friends. The show ran for six seasons and starred three Cox Friends co-stars: Lisa Kudrow, Jennifer Aniston and Matthew Perry.
Perry appeared as a guest star in the fifth season of the episode "Like a Diamond." He photographed Sam, the man whom Jules clashed with while trying to find her wedding ring that slipped while driving. In exchange for Sam forgetting about the damage to the car, Jules agrees to go with him on a date. Perry is funny and charming - Chandler is basically older and more confident.

In 2012, Matthew Perry returned to television in Go On, a sitcom created by Scott Silverie, who worked as a writer and executive producer at Friends. Apart from Matthew Perry, Tony Award-winning series Laura Benanti, Tyler James Williams, aka Chris from Everyone Hates Chris, Harold and Kumar John Chu - to name a few - starred. Perry filmed the sports radio presenter, Ryan King, pressured by his boss (Cho) to join a support group as he tried to move forward after his late wife's death. There he meets a strange group of people and reluctantly admits that treatment may not be a bad thing at all. Go On was an honest comedy that thrived in a sad and happy atmosphere with a taste of absurdity like a community. Unfortunately, the show was canceled after only one season.

Matthew Perry is a funny guy. Most of his roles were in comedy - whether TV or film, and his role in Friends as Sarcasm King Chandler Bing largely identified him. The bottom line, you see Matthew Perry, you expect him to be funny and lovely. That's what it is. That's why his role in The Good Wife, and its sub-series The Good Fight, is so refreshing and amazing.

Perry appeared several times in both shows, portraying Mike Christiva, a lawyer and former Republican candidate for governor, working for the U.S. Department of Justice and using all sorts of dirty schemes to get his way. It is evil through and through, which means that for the first time you can watch Matthew Perry without seeing Chandler.

The comedy drama Studio 60 on the Sunset Strip, a short-term behind-the-scenes look at a comedy fantasy TV series similar to Saturday Night Live, was Matthew Perry's first television role after friends Aaron Sorkin.The show received mixed reviews and was particularly panned by television comedians.However, it has received a new Rotten Tomatoes rating and is up for several Emmy Awards.Bradley Whitford, Amanda Pitt, Sarah Paulson, Steve Webber, and Matthew Perry were among the main cast members of Studio 60.Perry portrayed Matt Albee, the fantasy show's newly promoted executive producer and lead writer.for the Satellite Awards, Matthew Perry is up for best actor in a drama series.

One of the greatest and most influential television series of all time is Aaron Sorkin's award-winning political drama The West Wing.The Writers Guild of America ranks The West Wing as the tenth best television series for writing.From 1999 to 2006, the show ran for seven seasons.Matthew Perry, a star of Friends, made three appearances as Joe Quincy in The West Wing in 2003.Joe Quincey was a Republican lawyer who worked for Bartlett's Democratic administration as assistant White House counsel.Quincy was instrumental in negotiating the retirement of a Supreme Court judge and uncovered a scandal involving the vice president.Matthew Perry was nominated twice for the Primetime Emmy Award for best guest actor in a drama series for his performance.

In 2006, Matthew Perry starred in the TV film Ron Clark's story, which is based on real-life teacher Ron Clark. Directed by Ronda Heinz, director of the critically acclaimed film Children of a Lesser God, Ron Clarke's story stars Matthew Perry as a lavish teacher who leaves his small town to teach at a public school in New York City.

Students at the school were soon found to be segregated according to potential although the principal intended to appoint him to the honours category, Clark chose to take the most disadvantaged class. Through various trials and tribulations, Clark was able to reach out to his students and prepare them for life. Matthew Perry was nominated for Golden Globe and Emmy for his performance.

Fans of Friends are busy after the reunion episode screened on the health of the actor Matthew Perry, Chandler, who was quiet and sparsely spoken throughout the episode!

A source close to Matthew Perry told The Sun that his mystery during the episode was the result of emergency dental surgery he needed hours before filming the reunion episode.

Remarks on the episode Friends: The Reunion.. A real relationship between the two protagonists and changing the tone of talking about homosexuality

Kevin Bright, one of the series' writers, also revealed that Matthew Perry's state of health is good, Valla: "I think he's fine, his word, it's great to see him again, and what people say is what people say, I don't have anything to say about it, but it was great to see. I think it's very funny in the show. "

He continued: "He looks stronger and better since the last time I saw him, and excited to move forward."

The episode brought back special memories for the audience of Friends after the heroes of the series came together again after many years, restoring memories of the series and revealing the scenes.

The guest list included a number of celebrities, including David Beckham, Justin Bieber, bts, James Corden, Cindy Crawfrod, Lady Gaga, Elliot Gold, Kate Harrington, Larry Hankin, Mindy Kaling, Thomas Lennon, Christina Pickles, Tom Slick, James ick, MagGee Wheeller, Reiler and Reese wespoon

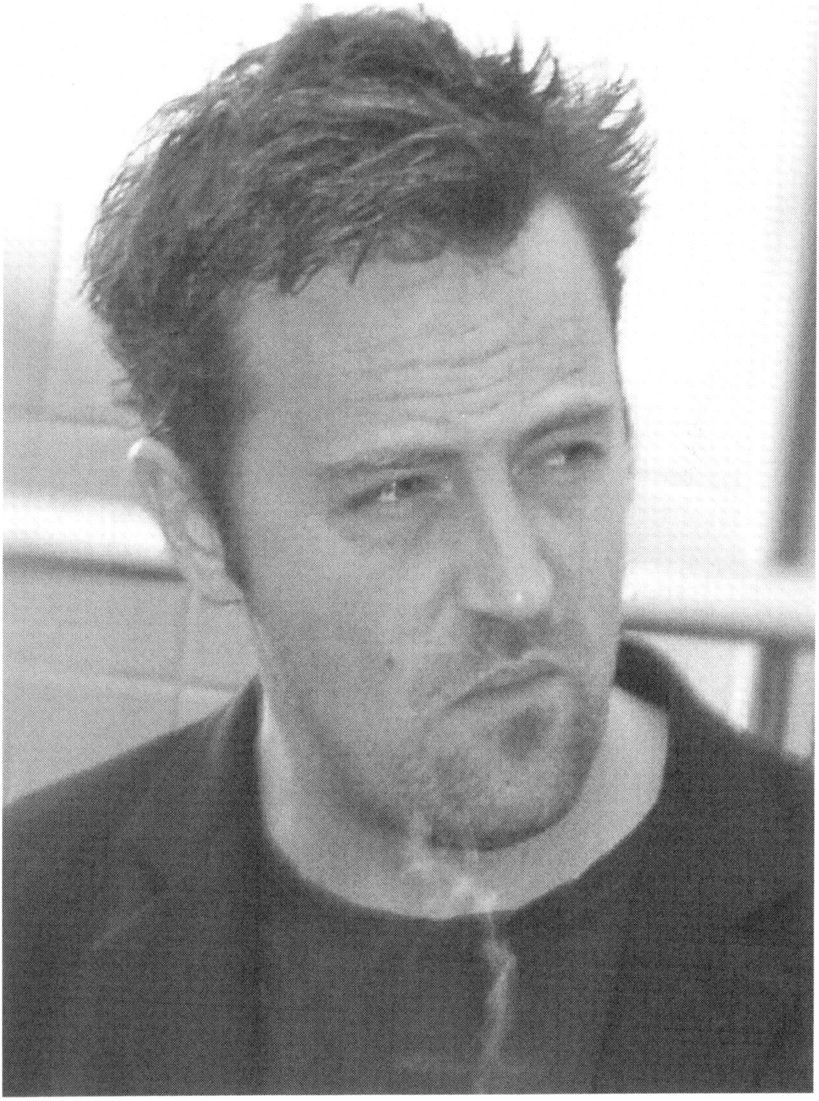

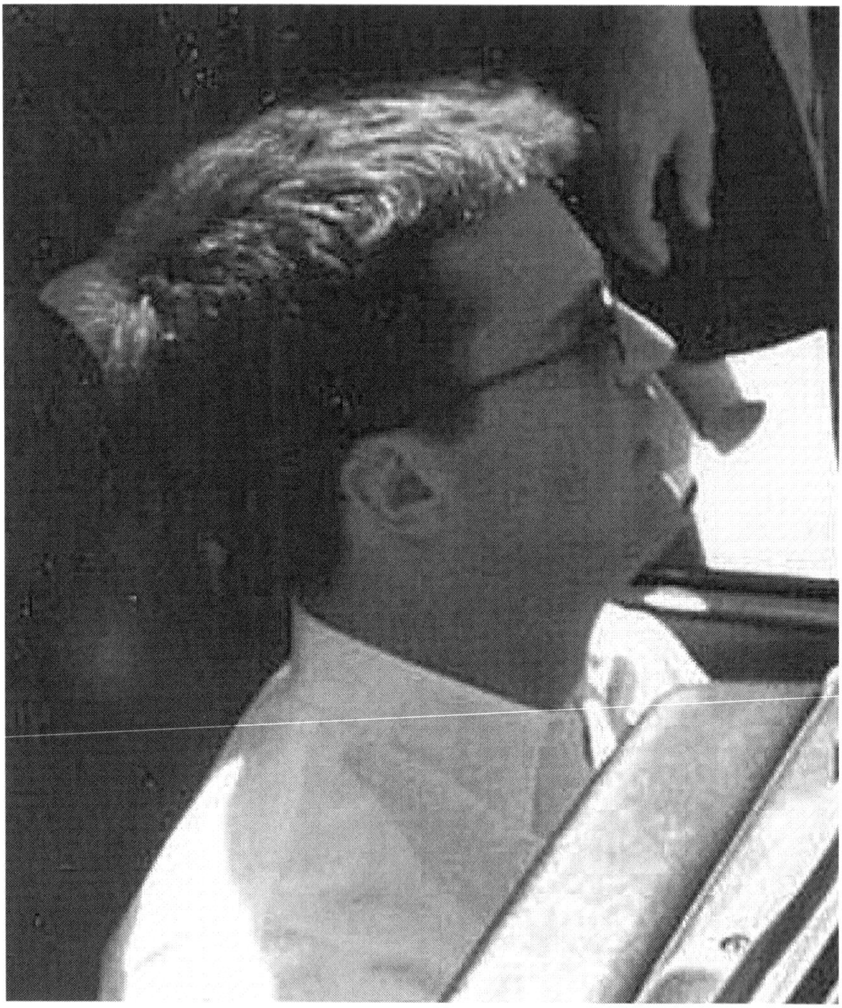

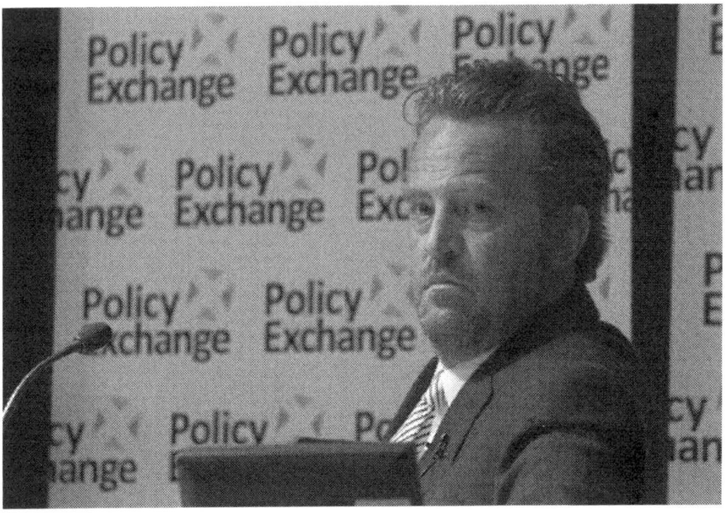
Policy
Exchange

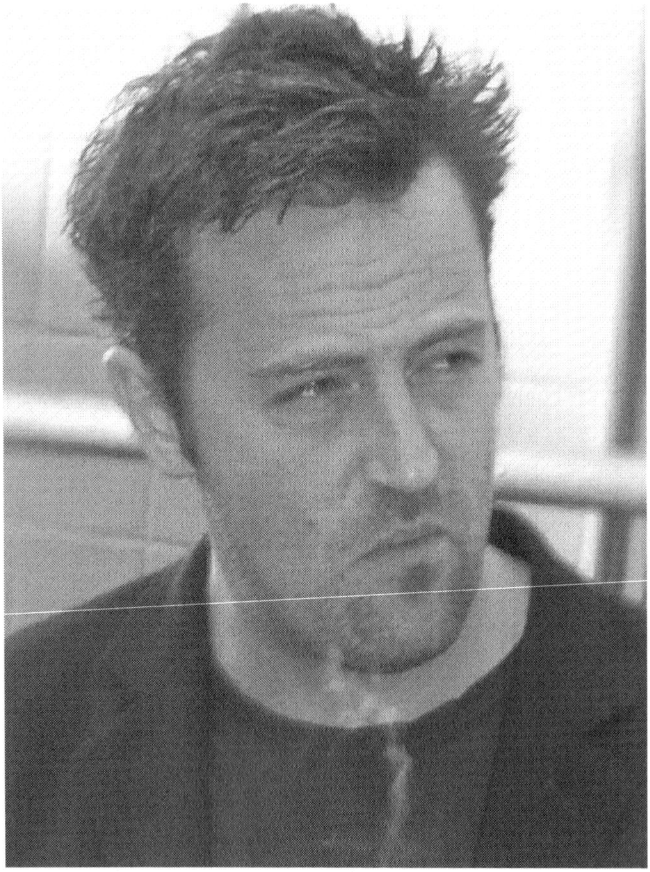

Made in the USA
Las Vegas, NV
28 October 2022